About the Author

My parents are from the East End, mother an artist and father an insurance clerk, decided to raise the family in the countryside and have a different pace of life. My restlessness of living in a small Cotswold town with big dreams and a vivid imagination led me to move to Greater Manchester where I discovered a bigger world, most importantly myself. Following inner spirit, I started my own business in holistic therapies and fate brought me back home again where in the most unexpected circumstances I met the person who inspired me to write.

Victoria Day-Joel

Poetry Inspired by Oliver Fantasy and Friendship

Olympia Publishers
London

www.olympiapublishers.com

OLYMPIA PAPERBACK EDITION

A CIP catalogue record for this title is
available from the British Library.

ISBN: 978-1-78830-186-2

First Published in 2018

Olympia Publishers
60 Cannon Street
London
EC4N 6NP

Printed in Great Britain

Dedication

Dedicated to Oliver, through our friendship I lived every word. Thank you.

Acknowledgements

Becky Brough Photography
Sue Mortin Astrologer

My living dream is the one I'm with is the only one I
will fantasise about, my one true desire
I know who you are.

You can only seek inspiration from something that moves you. This is the real me, a creative person expressing a world of internal juxtaposition from inner torment to true love's deepest desires through writing, in poetry. Meeting you has stirred me, I've come out of myself, is this what it is all about? Writing this to get it out into the world, my life's purpose to meet you, be inspired, become a writer, a creative. Well, now is the time to express myself.

I've always had romantic notions but never found my knight in shining armour, perhaps this time it will be different, we don't know each other well enough but I know I already want to get to know you.

The Calling

You will capture my imagination
Where my mind is engaged my heart will follow
My eyes are yours, I'll lead you to the depths of my soul
And through your dark eyes I can see inside
I will honour your light and embrace your dark
Nothing is hidden when we are together
You've touched me from within
I'm encapsulated by your beauty.

Love has the ability to see through judgement, colour and
boundaries, rational thought replaced with endorphins of
happiness, a spellbinding blindness

One Day

Each day we learn more about one other
the more I get to know you the more I like you
Our stories of the past are special memories of which
I hope we will be sharing the same ones together some
day.

*I'm starting to hear your voice in my head when I'm not
with you*

I Feel You

A gaze into your eyes is entering the depths of a deep
ocean, there are so many reasons why I want to get to
know you, be with you, see you, touch you, feel you.
When you speak, I will always listen, I will always take
time out for you, my attention is with you, I can't get
enough of looking into your eyes, thank you for making
me happy when I'm with you.
You take my mind into another dimension, I'm in love
with your mind, we talk about the universe, we talk about
music, we could talk all day if we wanted to, I dream
about you all day because I want to be with you.

*I consulted my friend Sue, an astrologer, to seek spiritual
guidance. Something I can't explain is happening to me, I
need to know what is my connection with Oliver?*
*"His Venus is conjunct your midheaven acting as your
muse."*
*When I'm with you there is nowhere I would rather be, no-
one I would rather see, you are my destiny!*

Tea Break

Morning is coffee, tea and a pinch of frivolity
We laugh at absurdities, share humour and stories

Discussing symptoms, solutions and society
With our spreadsheets, shared numbers and stationery

We are driven, work hard and have empathy, not taking
for granted
We're achieving, heading to where we want to be

I know I've got a good friend beside me
And will look back and feel blessed I shared good times in
your company.

Higher Realms

Our shared space was filled with a relaxed synchronicity
We were touched by our angels on a higher frequency
We don't go with everyone else's flow, it's an energy from
above
Who needs to fit in when we fit perfectly in joint
simplicity.

*After work we visited the local picture house, something
powerful happened when I looked at you, it was more than
a cinematic experience.*

Chemistry

That split-second glance was heaven
You've embodied a sexual power that pulls me to you,
It's strong and blinding I can't take my eyes off you
So intense I can't always look at you,
Like a lightning bolt out of nowhere
Can this even be real?

*Would love ruin our beautiful friendship or is love born
from a beautiful friendship? I believe in the latter, of
course I do.*
*From afar, your demeanour is a sexy darkness that I see
as passion, hypnotic eyes pulling me in deeper, your voice
sends me to a place that's just you and I where nothing
else matters, when I look at you I instinctively know how
you feel, do you feel it too?*

Like Me

I know you are deep like me
I know you seek passion like me
I know you're a free spirit like me.

I believe we are to be but have I lost touch with reality?
I believe everything happens for a reason, for our soul's
growth, when the timing is right for us both 'we' will
happen. I will not lose faith and believe dreams will come
true, my intention is set, I daydream and fantasise we're
already together, it feels so real, when will this happen?
Emotions running high and fantasies running wild.

Sweet Distraction

The way you look, the way you speak
Can distract me, sending feelings to peak
It's hard to resist your alluring charm
As you're in my head with no qualms
Nobody knows these feelings inside
Yes, we're friends but there's something I hide
You make me laugh you make me smile
It's nice when these thoughts stay a while
A warming glow of friendship speaks
Beneath the surface emotions run deep.

The face we put out to the world isn't who we are, the light within us shines through from our eyes, we can see our souls, but do we feel dead or alive?
If we bear all, our light casts a shadow, who really knows the shadow of ourselves, our deepest desires, fears and fantasies?
Who is willing to open up their heart and soul to another to show who they really are? Without ego, without holding back through fear of judgement or rejection, we would be

free. This is a time of deep transformation where I'm allowing my shadow self to come out, this is who I am, let me express who I am, I am open to you, I want to show you who I am. I am alive, you have brought me to life.

Lights On

Life is light and dark
We are not how others see us to be
Want us to be or expect us to be
I want you to know the real me

I'm starting to feel you know me best
We are multi-faceted, have many layers
But how far do we go and how deep do we show?
You've changed me, I'm not afraid to expose, I'm all for
you to see.

*I'm wondering, without you how would my dreams come
to life?*
*Today was one of those light bulb moments, an exciting
opportunity for your artwork and my writing has occurred
out of nowhere.*

Inspiration

You have unlocked the door to creation, third eye open, a
light, a vision
Open to express thoughts on a new page
Process black and white to colour
Bring the page to life with your artistic vision
Thank you for being my inspiration.

*At the moment I have no permanent abode, currently
residing in an over 55s' warden assisted community
maisonette, which is a short stay room for friends and
relatives or local residents, my short stay has been
extended somewhat so it's a case of keeping a low profile.
My room has a bed with a shower in the corner, porcelain
ducks sit on the window ledge. Across the hall are WCs
and walking aids, a utility room, separate kitchen and
communal lounge with many high back chairs, a dusty
dart board, numerous books and a hi-fi unit from the 90s.
Note it is now 2017!
I'm in bed and been thinking of you in a way that feels
more than just friends, so I start writing and I can't stop,*

later I fall asleep and it seems I carried those thoughts into my dream and woke at 1.30 am to your call on my mobile phone. My heart skips a beat, I answer and whisper whilst walking across the hall into the residents' lounge as there are people sleeping in the room upstairs, being careful not to wake them. It's pitch black outside, there are no curtains drawn, just a room full of chairs, I'm still under the influence of my dream and a bit shocked at the timing. I'm shivery but my dream has given me confidence and bravery and I'm thinking if ever there was a time to announce how I feel then surely it feels like now, so I tell you 'I've been writing and what I'm about to read is how I feel about you.' So here goes now is the time to announce my feelings to you through erotic poetry but first I say, "This might blow your mind."

Fantasy

I'll knock at your door in the finest female form
Smooth stockings caress my legs with my fleshy thighs
exposed to touch
Suspender belt tight like the grip of your hand around my
waist
Soft black lace cups my breasts, only my coat for cover
In anticipation, blood pumping, can you hear my heart
beating?

You open the door, our eyes meet
Dark and deep like the brandy in my veins
We do not speak one touch is enough to connect us

Unbutton from the bottom to the top
Feel the curves as you move upwards until you release my
coat

Come closer, touch my lipstick red lips, press your lips to
mine
Your body presses into me tightly, I pull your hair

I can smell you, I want to taste you, can I handle you?
Your firm tattooed arms move around my body

I run my fingers down your back, do you feel alive? Do
you want me?
You've entered my mind, I'm ready for you to enter my
body

Every push filtrating head to toe in a passionate embrace
The divine masculine and feminine meet.

*The following day I hand write my fantasy and send it in
the post to you as a surprise for your eyes, it feels old
fashioned and I like the thought of you reading it and
remembering some of the words and my voice as you read
it for the first time.*
*I didn't tell you that my mind didn't stop that weekend and
another fantasy was born, it stayed hidden as you told me
the following day you have started to see someone, so this
was to be kept under lock and key, so right now we are not
meant to be. This is the hidden Fantasy.*

Hidden Fantasy

I walk up your staircase by the flicker of candlelight and
the heady aroma of incense
Dressed in a black basque strapped to suspenders ready to
tease
You watch me from the end of your bed
I twist my long flowing hair to my nipples
My hands slide down my body, from the nape of my neck,
around my shoulders
And up and down my thighs. I rock my hips thinking
about being intimate with you.
I part my legs and lean my body over to the edge of the
bed but you still can't touch
I flick my hair back as I slowly move towards you, you
look cool and sexy, your eyes drawing me closer in, my
legs are locking either side of your body, the tease is too
much to take.
As I lower, you enter me, I press down at your arms,
moving slowly and deeply in a state of heavenly bliss, now
we are flowing like the rhythm of the tide.

Sea Escape

Did you take in the breeze as you looked out to sea?
Did you ever think it could be just you and me?
Having some time out on your own
Were you thinking of me back home
I liked the photo of the cave you explored one day
A room with a view for the pirate to stay
To relax and unwind from the busy world
Behind the scenes I still dream of being your girl.

*Last night was the best night I've had with someone of the
opposite sex without being in a relationship with them. I
can't tell you how I feel as you are with another, but as
friends we laughed we cried, looked into each other's eyes,
singing and dancing.*

Our Harmony

We speak of being wild and free through the whisky and
the brandy
You're a cowboy riding high in Tennessee
I'm a gypsy of the caves and waterways
Behind the door music is our harmony
Where our minds can escape from society
Through song and dance we express ourselves easily
Be whatever we want to be
We're technicoloured dream coats
Vibrant in frequency, making our own melody
If Saturday was my only memory
I could hold forever more in your company.

Déjà vu

Time is infinite, as is my deep longing for you
Am I in a parallel universe which only I can feel and
observe?
Between dimensions? Let me in on the other side
Have I been here before? It feels like déjà vu.

Alignment

A connection of minds runs deeper than physical attraction
I believe we've entered a soul journey through our eyes
Ignite fire add air, is a creative affair
Join Venus and midheaven
The universe is speaking through synchronicity
An inner knowing, we are to be in what capacity?
We are experiencing extra sensory
Will we be close physically
You and me, what is our destiny?

*Fate has brought a twist and turn, you are now back on
your own, another weekend when I feel amped up with no
release.*
*When we speak late at night, what are you thinking? If
you've been drinking I have been sleeping, if you are
sleeping I have been drinking, what else can I do? I send
you my poetry.*

Intimacy

Let intimacy embody us
Through eyes that burn deep within our souls
A place that knows no boundaries
Vulnerability is connection and beauty
An expression through physicality

One touch is electricity
Flowing through our bodies
Awakening the senses
So let's explore and begin this sacral journey.

Animal Magnetism

I'm imagining the intensity of our first touch
Pressed up so close I can smell you through your clothes
I want to rip them off, like an animal
Senses so strong
So intense I can't see you, just feel you
I need to be wild with you
Our tongues lock like our bodies soon
Skin on skin
Touch, me, taste me
Let me have some more
Legs apart and bare
Lock into me
Press and pull me
Pinch and tease me
I'm waiting for all of you
Turn me on with your teeth
Bite me, scratch me
This is raw instinct
Make love to me
Now caress me.

Passion

I feel passion so strong
I want to give you everything I've got
Nothing can reign me in
Intoxicate me I'll come alive
Touch me, hurt me
I need pleasure and pain
I know you're the same

Let me breathe your energy
So I can still feel you after I've gone
Distance will not change our chemistry

You're my desire, the fire within
I carry you in my heart
whether I'm with or without you
Always remember this, my baby.

Senses

Play with my senses, my darling
If I can't see you I will feel you harder
If I can't touch you I will want you closer
This is always how it has been
Dreams and a vivid imagination.

*If bliss I felt like this could be bottled I would hold you
forever*

*Day dreaming whilst walking back to the car after
finishing work, what else can I say, you looked sexy today.*

Pleasure

Erotic thoughts of you consume me
You are my number one fantasy
Lick me, tease me, suck on me and squeeze me
With these thoughts you can only please me.

*I've taken a trip away on Talamanca beach, feel renewed
in spirit,
however near or far you will be forever in my thoughts.*

Thinking

I'm thinking of you and what would your thoughts be
As if they are written on the page in front of me
Mine are filled with our friendship and fantasy
Rose tinted, blue skies of love and creativity
Expressing the gift your friendship has given me.

*I'm back to work but we are a larger office now, I can't
always say the words that I would say if it were just you
and I, we've had telepathic ability, now I'm not sure you
can hear me.*

Silence

When I can't talk to you I whisper in my mind the words I
want to say to you
Maybe you can hear them, maybe I just dream them
Maybe they swim around for a while until you feel them.

*You are a beautiful soul that is all I can see when I look at
you.*

Faultless

I'm finding it hard not to like everything about you
Even the crinkles under your eyes when tired make you
look rugged
When you're silent and moody your testosterone fuels fire
inside me
When you're angry I want to be the one who looks into
your eyes and holds your shoulders to calm you
Will I ever find a way to distance myself from your natural
beauty?

*We attended a wedding reception in style as resident
glampers, on that hazy day in July. My first camping
experience would be one to remember.*

Camping

On that crazy campsite night
You offered me your shelter
I needed you close and placed my arm across your
shoulder
Feeling your strong bicep with my head on your chest
How minds start to wander
We gently touch into a tease knowing we can't take it
further
Like a lucid dream this is a lovely drunken haze
Now reality is here which I've been dreaming of for weeks
and days
We fall asleep knowing friendship will remain
And wake to feel the same,
A natural touch with a loving friend
This becomes a memory of the first time we blurred
friendship with chemistry, my dear.

You're the warmth of the first ray of sunlight touching my
skin, come out of nowhere
Now I've felt you I don't want this to disappear

I believe writing comes from a place of pure love and
connection
If I'm still I can listen to my internal voice
Like the beauty of listening to a choir of angels
Or harmonies or bird song.

Radiate

My soul knows you're the one
Everything that I've ever wanted
My inner fire may breathe too strong
As feelings can't be contained for too long
So I let them out with creative expression
Live from the heart and radiate with passion.

See the Light

Does the light in your eyes shine solely for me?
Do the stars in the sky map the pathway I see?
The moon is my energy, the sun is your power
Eternal spirit glows by the hour.

Electric Rainbow

My pulse is an electric current
You are the conductor
Each day we are fusing together
It makes separation harder
So much energy bonds us stronger
In overdrive to the skies
Together we're an electric rainbow.

As good friends who work together we know our
boundaries but it's not always easy when your heart rules
your head. As time moves on, I still want you.

Caged Highway

My mind is a busy place like a heavy highway
With intermittent breathing space when you realise you
can look at the sky and breathe
My soul is connected to you and I can't let go
My heart is in a cage waiting for freedom
In the ether my mind is trying to connect to you through
the astral plane
Are we both going through the same bittersweet pain?
In a different way yet feel the same?
I think of you every day but cannot be with you in that
way.

Longing

Tears are falling for I am grieving for a love I long for that
I cannot have
In my mind and in my dreams I've already touched you, I
feel you in my heart
You were with another but now free and I'm still in
captivity
How long will it be? Or do I need to get back to reality?

Anchor

I'm overwhelmed by emotion
Swimming in sadness
Hold me and be my anchor
In calm waters
I'm far away in thought
Can't come down to earth
Bring me back
I'm too far out.

*Am I in a dangerous illusion, thoughts bringing pain and
confusion?*
How do I feel each day?
Like I live and breathe you
You're the oxygen that keeps me alive
If only you knew.

Mixed Up

For every high there is a low
For every thought there is a consequence
I choose attraction, I choose the fantasy
Some days I can't accept the reality

I'm living from the heart and it's you in my head
I've wanted you from the start so come share my bed
It's not that easy, our friendship is too strong
I want you forever in my life, one night is not long.

Imaginary Love Story

I am not like any other
But will you get to see my wonder
I'm sad inside without you near
Are we holding back through heads of fear?

My heart says yes but when's the time?
I want to ask, will you be mine?
Will we be more than friends?
Or a love story in my mind that never ends.

Flame in the Wind

My heart is not wrong,
I have to stay strong
You are the one I'm waiting for
When the timing is right
Sexual desire is passion that's fire
A flame from solid ground
Will burn stronger and brighter
Able to grow, be wild in the wind
Give warmth through light and dark
Forever will you burn in my heart
Let it be by my side,
come along for the ride
As this is just the start.

Dreaming

I've dreamt of crossing boundaries but friendship is reality
If we are to be then the universe will guide me
Work is our blessing with temptation beside me
I won't be ready until I know you really want me
For more than one night as I'm too open to sensitivity
You are the head, I am the heart
So where do I start?
I'll continue to be wrapped up in you
I will always adore you and my wildest fantasies will all
be about you
With time grows deep affection and care
For love and friendship, I will always be there.

Friendship Entwined

I sit with my thoughts and they always come back to you
A friendship so strong I feel I really know you
The physical gateway is not yet open,
There's a sacred garden waiting to blossom

We have the key but when will it be?
It has not been determined, our destiny
We are engaged in neutral position
One turn changes reality

Is it right or wrong, who can say?
Will we be able to work together each day?
Jealousy fear and sadness portray
If we both don't feel the same way

Change may come if we are to be near
The material side I do not hold dear
Compared to the price to pay
Of moving on as lovers in union one day.

This is the morning after a night out of music and entertainment. I wake to the sound of you rolling out of your sleeping bag from the couch as you gave me your bed to sleep in last night. The melody is you strumming your guitar downstairs as I lay upstairs singing, just thinking how I would love to experience this every day, it's 8am, a breath of fresh air has swept inside me.

Knowing You

Knowing you is feeling close like we're each other's
family
You know how I think better than most
Feeling comfort with you is like wearing my favourite new
clothes
That I don't want to take off
When I see your face the last piece of puzzle has fitted into
place
We see beyond the mirror but we like to look into it too!

Tiger's Eye

Only you have taken my mind to places its not been
To the top of the mountain, to the valley below
With no mask no fear, we go deeper
We shine like tigers' eyes and see clearer
The world is ours to conquer
As each day foundations grow stronger
You know what you like, not a follower
A lone wolf, together we are warriors.

*It's Hallowe'en weekend I'm staying in a B&B 150 miles
from home to visit a good friend, it's 1am I've had too
much to drink and try to phone just to hear your voice.
You're asleep, I'm dressed as a vampire and not long ago
walked from the Hallowe'en party to the next inn with the
Little Mermaid, Tarzan and Mary Poppins. We sing into a
hairbrush and dance around, meeting 'civilians', one of
whom has taken a shine to me. Later on we have a lock-in,
said civilian puts his coat round me to keep me warm and
pulls me close, we kiss, but now I find myself navigating
through emotional turbulence until I disappear into a taxi
into the night wondering why I feel so numb.*

Shadows

The light stings my eyes
The dark fills the skies that are inside my head
Maybe it hurts because he wasn't you
Maybe my thoughts won't become true
When time moves on do we stay still or change ways?
Another day balancing the scales, they weigh heavy today.

*As the nights have turned darker it seems my thoughts
have gone that way too, it hurts knowing I can't be with
you but I live through light and dark.*

Ride

I don't have a handle on my emotions
Will you ride the waves with me and taste my tears?
Will you hold me when I need you to feel my fears?
Can you contain my fire when I burn for you?
Touch me through the flame
I'm a roller coaster up and down, a runaway train
Shine your light, bring me down to solid ground.

Breathe

Please breathe for me
It hurts being so deep
I need someone to feel for me
When I'm numb where does the pain go?
Who is in control?

*My thoughts can be nebulous but you are always
somewhere.*

Compass

My internal compass is pointing towards you
Is it me that moves or is the world just spinning?
I know where I want to go but I can't get there right now
I'll just keep spinning.

Satellite

I'm floating in the sky like a satellite
Destined to come back to you
Hear my words in the wind
Feel my guidance deep within
You know my answer
But what is the question?
You're moving through me as sensory energy in motion.

Constellations

The stars are my guide
The moon lights the way
We're strong like the tide
Emotions run high
Water it cleanses
Let it wash over me.

*We've had a festive weekend away in London with friends,
I can't tell you how good you look or touch you like I want
to.*

White

Snow has fallen in the city
But I'm dazzled by your white light
You wearing a white shirt with the top button undone
Your dark features are the backdrop to the night sky
Spirit of passion lights the path to my heart.

Holding On

Can we hold one perfect moment that stands still in our
timeline?
When a smile through eyes wears no disguise
A touch of lips pressed lightly in sensual anticipation
Our hearts beat like the bang of a drum vibrating louder
and harder
Mind and bodies aligning for the first time.

I had too much to drink last night, it's the small hours of
Christmas Day
A time when loved ones come together
You're not far away but we are apart over this season
I would do so much to be with you
if the snow fell and mountains moved
I would still try to find a way
For now I imagine what it would be like.

I Imagine

Touching your lips and not being able to let go
Your chest as the perfect resting place bringing comfort
Our hearts as radar beams so we will never be lost again
Your eyes holding me in the light forever.

Wide Eyes

As I look in the mirror my eyes are alive
I see the world inside them
Green of the lush trees
Brown of the earthly woodland
The depth of the ocean
I have and feel it all inside me
Connection with mother earth
Guided by spirit, blessed to be
Tonight, I feel you beside me
From the heart and in spirit
Goodnight my beauty.

Always follow your heart, this is my place to start.
With friendship a fantasy was born.